誠 MAKOTO

e-zine for learners of Japanese

ご 購入
ありがとう
ございます。

Thank you so much
for your purchase!

We recently began offering lifetime memberships for Makoto+. When we started Makoto magazine — 4 years ago next month!! — we had several subscribers ask for a lifetime deal. (I love lifetime deals too!) While totally committed to the project, at the time I didn't feel right offering a lifetime option without knowing that we would be able to keep it up.

Now, almost 4 years later, not only have we continued the magazine, we've greatly expanded its monthly content and added Makotoplus.com with its weekly lessons, bonus content, and freebie downloads. In other words, I feel like we can now offer a lifetime deal that is truly an incredible value for any student of Japanese.

Please read about this offer here:

https://makotoplus.com/lifetime-makoto/

Thank you!
Clay & Yumi

P.S. We are including QR codes so you can easily scan and hear audio directly from the e-zine. Let us know if you have other ideas for improvement!

The cover says, 読んでね *yonde ne*, which means, "Read it, won't you!"

WHO ARE WE?

Nearly two decades ago, Clay & Yumi began **TheJapanesePage.com**, one of the Internet's oldest and largest *free* Japanese instructional sites with hundreds of free articles for beginners of Japanese.

They also maintain **TheJapanShop.com**, a webstore specializing in materials to help learners of Japanese.

Have any questions or comments? Contact us at **help@thejapanshop.com**

In this Issue:

2

LAUGHS, JOKES, RIDDLES, AND PUNS

友人（ゆうじん）の宣言（せんげん）：

「もうギャンブルはやらない。賭（か）けてもいい。」

A friend's declaration:

"I've given up gambling. You can bet on it!"

Scan for Recording

Vocabulary:

ジョーク *jo-ku*—a joke

友人の宣言 *yuujin no sengen*—declaration of a friend [友人 (friend) + の (of; modifier) + 宣言 (declaration; proclamation)]

「」—(quotation marks; " ")

もう *mou*—(not) anymore; already [shows he has already stopped]

ギャンブル *gyanburu*—gambling

は *wa*—(indicates the sentence topic; adds emphasis)

やらない *yaranai*—do not; don't do [plain negative form of やる (to do; to play (game); to perform)]

賭けてもいい *kakete mo ii*—(you) can bet (on it) [from 賭ける (to bet; to gamble); ~てもいい means "can; may; is okay; is all right to"; how to form: Verb て-form + もいい]

VOCABULARY

Learn Useful Words, Phrases, and Sayings

Scan for Recording

<うま あ>
馬が合う

uma ga au

to get along (with someone); hit it off

ⓘ Use this when you are on the same wavelength as someone else.

Literally, "to suit a horse." This idiom comes from how a rider synchronizes his breathing to the horse's. People find it easier to get along with certain people rather than to others. This is similar to the relationship of riders and horses. You can also say "〜と馬が合わない" (don't get along with~)

EXAMPLE SENTENCE:

彼女とは、初めて会ったときから馬が合うと感じた。

kanojo to wa, hajimete atta toki kara uma ga au to kanjita.

Upon meeting her for the first time, I just knew we'd hit it off.

Example Sentence

VOCABULARY:

彼女 *kanojo*—she

と *to*—with (her) [Example: 私は Aさんと馬が会う。]

は *wa*—[It's a contrast marker more than a topic marker, emphasizing 彼女

Vocabulary Continued

and contrasting others whom the speaker might not get along with so well.]

初めて *hajimete*—the first time

会ったとき *atta toki*—when (we) met [会った (met) + とき (when (we met))]

から *kara*—from (the first meeting); since (we met)

馬が合う *uma ga au*—to get along; to hit it off [馬 (horse) + が (subject marker) + 会う (to suit)]

と *to*—quotation marker [quoting the preceding phrase; consider と as "that" as in, "I felt <u>that</u> I would get along with her."]

感じた *kanjita*—felt; had a feeling [plain past form of 感じる (to feel; to sense)]

Aichi 愛知

Japanese: 愛知県 *aichi ken*
Capital: 名古屋 Nagoya
Population: 7,552,873 (October 1, 2019)

DID YOU KNOW?

A densely populated prefecture with Toyota headquartered in its namesake city, Toyota City. Nagoya is Japan's fourth largest city. The prefectural symbol depicts the rising sun over the waves while also being a stylized あいち, the hiragana for Aichi.

PLACES TO SEE:

- Tour of the **Toyota car factory** in the city of Toyota.

- **Port of Nagoya Public Aquarium**—a large aquarium.

- **The four castles** in Nagoya, Okazaki, Toyohashi, and Inuyama.

- **Meiji Village** is an open-air museum exhibiting the architecture of the Meiji period (1868-1912).

- **Kourankei**—a beautiful valley located in eastern Toyota City. It is famous for having over 4,000 momiji (maple) trees. A must see in the fall when the leaves change colors.

FAMOUS FOR:

- **The three unifiers: Oda Nobunaga, Toyotomi Hideyoshi, and Tokugawa Ieyasu** were all born in what is now Aichi prefecture.

- Home of **Toyota, Brother, Noritake, Makita,** and many other large corporations.

- **Inuyama Castle**—perhaps the oldest still standing castle, dating back to 1440. Most of the castle is in its original condition.

- **Nagoya Station**—the world's largest train station.

「ガチ」

「*Gachi*」

Scan for Recording

　ガチは、「本気、真面目、本当に」という意味で使います。元々は、相撲の世界で使っている「ガチンコ」という言葉でした。「ガチンコ」というのは、力士と力士が勢いよくぶつかり合った時にでる「ガチン」という音から、「真剣勝負」という言い方になりました。ガチは「真剣勝負、真面目に」という意味以外に「最高だ、本物だ」という意味でも使われます。「あのアーティストはガチだ。」つまり、「あのアーティストは、本物だ。」という意味になります。

Gachi is used to mean "earnest, seriousness, truly".

Originally, it's from "*gachinko*" which is used in the world of sumo.
The word "*gachinko*" comes from the "*gachin*" sound that is produced

Continued

when two *sumo* wrestlers collide with each other vigorously, and became a way of saying "a serious match." *Gachi* is used not only to mean "a serious match," or "seriously," but also to mean "the best," or "genuine." "That artist is *gachi*." That would mean "That artist is the real deal."

Vocabulary

語源 etymology; origin of a word

ガチは *gachi* [ガチ (*gachi*) + は (indicates the sentence topic)]

「」(quotation marks; " ")

本気 earnest; seriousness; truth; sanctity

真面目 seriousness; sobriety; honest; steady

本当に truly; really; for real

という意味 such a meaning [という (is used to define, describe, and generally just talk about the thing itself) + 意味 (sense; meaning)]

で by; with [indicates means of action]

使います use [ます/polite form of 使う (to use)]

元々は originally; traditionally speaking [元々 (originally; from the start) + は (adds emphasis)]

相撲の世界で in the world of *sumo* [相撲 (*sumo*; *sumo* wrestling) + の (of; modifier) + 世界 (the world; world) + で (in; indicates the location of action)]

使っている is/are using; use; is/are used [ている-form of 使う (to use) which is used to describe a continuous action; how to form: Verb て-form + いる]

「ガチンコ」という言葉 the word "*gachinko*"; the word called "*gachinko*" [「ガチンコ」("*gachinko*") + という (called) + 言葉 (word; term)]

でした was; were [polite past tense marker, typically used with nouns and な-adjectives; how to form: Noun/な-adjective (stem form) + でした]

というのは is; means [expression; conjunction]

Vocabulary Continued

力士と力士が　*sumo* wrestler and *sumo* wrestler [力士 (*sumo* wrestler) + と　(and) + 力士 (*sumo* wrestler) + が　(identifies who performs the action)]

勢いよく　vigorously; with great force; energetically

ぶつかり合った　collided; clashed [plain past form of ぶつかり合う　(to collide; to clash)]

時にでる「ガチン」という音　the sound "*gachin*" that is produced when [時 (when; at this time; how to form: Verb (casual form) + 時) + に　(indicates the specific time) + でる　(to be produced) + 「ガチン」("*gachin*") + という　(that; called) + 音　(sound)]

から　from

真剣勝負　serious match; game played in real earnest; "fighting with real swords" [真剣 (serious; earnest) + 勝負　(match; game; contest)]

「真剣勝負」という言い方　a way of saying "a serious match" [「真剣勝負」("serious match") + という　(that says) + 言い方　(way of saying (something); wording; phrasing; expression)]

になりました　became [に　(expresses the result of change) + なりました　(polite past form of なる　(to become; to turn))]

「真剣勝負、真面目に」"a serious match" or "seriously" [「」 (quotation marks; " ") + 真剣勝負 (serious match) + 真面目に　(seriously; soberly; solemnly)]

「真剣勝負、真面目に」という意味以外に　other than to mean "a serious match" or "seriously" [「真剣勝負、真面目に」("a serious match" or "seriously") + という　(is used to define, describe, and generally just talk about the thing itself) + 意味　(meaning; sense; significance) + 以外に　(other than; with the exception of; but; except)]

「最高だ、本物だ」"the best" or "genuine" [「」 (quotation marks; " ") + 最高だ (the best; 最高 (best; finest; supreme) + だ　(casual form of です　(be; is))) + 本物だ　(genuine; 本物 (genuine article; real thing; real deal) + だ　(casual form of です　(be; is)))]

Vocabulary Continued

「最高だ、本物だ」という意味でも使われます is also used to mean "the best" or "genuine" [「最高だ、本物だ」("the best" or "genuine") + という (is used to define, describe, and generally just talk about the thing itself) + 意味 (meaning; sense; significance) + でも (but; also; as well) + 使われます (polite passive positive form of 使う (to use))]

「あのアーティストはガチだ。」"That artist is *gachi*." [「」(quotation marks; " ") + あの (that; those; the) + アーティスト (artist) + は (indicates the sentence topic) + ガチ (*gachi*) + だ (casual form of です (be; is))]

つまり (I) mean; in other words; that is; which is to say; so; in fact

「あのアーティストは、本物だ。」"That artist is the real deal." [あの (that; those; the) + アーティスト (artist) + は (indicates the sentence topic) + 本物 (real deal; real thing; genuine article) + だ (casual form of です (be; is))]

という意味になります it means that; mean; it comes to mean [という (that; called) + 意味 (meaning; sense) + に (expresses the result of change) + なります (ます/polite form of なる (to become; to turn; come to))]

ANIME / MANGA PHRASE

Surprise your Japanese friends with these phrases

Please see the sound files for the pronunciation

しょくげき
食戟のソーマ

はい と
「入ったからには、てっぺん取るんで。」

ゆきひらそうま
幸平創真のセリフ

Scan for Recording

shokugeki no so-ma

「*haitta kara ni wa, teppen toru n de.*」

yukihira souma no serifu

Food Wars!
"Now that I'm in, I'm going to take the top."
Line from Yukihira Souma

VOCABULARY

The context is a student is entering a new school and vows to become popular.

食戟 *shokugeki*—food wars; food competitions [食 (food; foodstuff; meal) + 戟 (weapon; arms; long-handled Chinese spear)]

の *no*—of; 's [modifier]

ANIME / MANGA PHRASE

Surprise your Japanese friends with these phrases

Continued

ソーマ *so-ma*—Sōma [main character of the anime Food Wars!]

「」 —(quotation marks; " ")

入った *haitta*—entered; joined (school) [plain past form of 入る (to enter; to go in; to join)]

からには *kara ni wa*—now that; since; so long as; because ~ [how to form: Verb (casual, past) + からには]

てっぺん *teppen*—top; peak; summit

てっぺん取るんで *teppen toru n de*—to take the top [casual way to say トップを取る (take the top; トップ (top) + を (indicates the direct object of action) + 取る (to take)) which sounds masculine; ~んで is used to show more emotion or emphasis]

幸平創真のセリフ *yukihira souma no serifu*—line from Yukihira Souma [幸平創真 (Yukihira Souma) + の (of; from; 's; modifier) + セリフ (one's lines; speech; words)]

Kobayashi Issa 小林一茶
こばやしいっさ

夕ざくら　けふ*も 昔 に

成にけり

Haiku Audio

yuuzakura / kyou mo mukashi ni / nari ni keri*

Evening cherry blossoms | now today also | has become the distant past

* Read the old style けふ as "kyou"

Explanation

Explanation:

夕方に 桜 を見ています。今日という日も過ぎ去って 昔 になりました。

Watching the cherry blossoms in the evening. Even this day has gone and became the distant past.

夕ざくら night cherry blossom; cherry blossoms at night; watching cherry blossoms in the evening

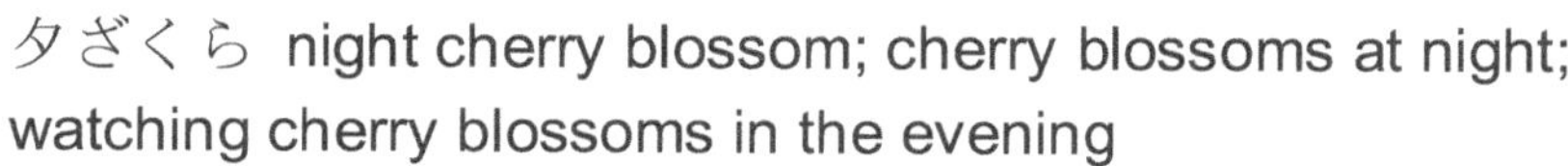

13

Vocabulary Continued

けふ today [old Japanese for "今日 (today)"; prior to WWII, some Japanese words were read differently than what the hiragana would suggest. けふ is pronounced "kyou". For more on this, see **"The Makoto Letter #7"** in the Bonus Content section on MakotoPlus.com]

も even

昔に into olden days; in days gone by; to the old days [昔 (olden days; former times; days gone by) + に (indicates the specific time)]

成にけり turned; became; it was [indicates one's personal recollection about something]

夕方に in the evening [夕方 (evening; dusk) + に (in; specifies time)]

桜 cherry blossom; cherry tree

を (indicates the direct object of action)

見ています is/are watching [ています-form of 見る (to watch; to see; to view) which is used to describe an ongoing action; how to form: Verb て-form + います]

今日という日も even this day; even the day called today [今日 (today; this day) + という (called; that) + 日 (day; days) + も (even)]

過ぎ去って passed by and; gone and [て-form of 過ぎ去る (pass by; elapse) which is used to connect to the next phrase, creating the meaning of "and"]

昔になりました became the distant past [昔 (distant past; former times; old days; in days of old) + になりました (polite past form of になる (become; come to; turn out))]

小林一茶 Kobayashi Issa (1763 – 1828) [A Japanese poet and lay Buddhist priest. He is known as simply Issa, a pen name which means "Cup-of-tea". He is regarded as one of the four Haiku masters in Japan.]

14

KANJI SPOTLIGHT

Learning kanji one character at a time.

JLPT N5 Kanji

友

On: ユウ

Kun: とも

Meaning: friend

Hint: A picture of a friend giving another friend a hand.

Audio of Readings

This kanji is often used with words dealing with friendliness.

Stroke Order:

友 一 ナ 方 友

Examples:

とも
友だち friends; a friend

ゆうじょう
友情 friendship

ゆうこうこく
友好国 a friendly nation

とちゅう　　とも　　　　あ
途中で友だちに会いました。

tochuu de tomodachi ni aimashita.

On the way, I ran into a friend.

[*tochuu* is a very useful word meaning "on the way" or "in the midst of" and is used both spatially and temporally.]

Audio of Example

VOCABULARY:

途中 *tochuu*—on the way; en route

途中で *tochuu de*—in the middle of ~; on the way [describes an action that is taking place and interrupted by other action]

JLPT N5 Kanji

友

On: ユウ

Kun: とも

Meaning: friend

Hint: A picture of a friend giving another friend a hand.

Audio of Readings

Vocabulary Continued

友だち *tomodachi*—friend; companion

に *ni*—into [expresses the object of the verb]

会いました *aimashita*—met [polite past form of 会う (to meet; to encounter; to see)]

もう

ABOUT:

Don't confuse this with the shorter (in sound) も which means "also." This もう means **"already"** (something has *already* happened) or, with a negative verb, **"not anymore"** (done in the past but not *now*).

HOW TO USE:

■ Since もう isn't tied to a specific verb or noun, it can be used in various positions in the sentence, but it is usually at the beginning of the sentence. Also, with the "not anymore" meaning, finish with a negative verb.

EXAMPLES:

<u>もう</u>食べました。

(I) have <u>**already**</u> eaten.

[already | ate]

Example 1

<u>もう</u>酒を飲みません。

(I) don't drink *sake* <u>**anymore**</u>.

[not anymore | *sake* | don't drink]

Example 2

Continued

VOCABULARY:

もう *mou*—already; (not) anymore

食べました *tabemashita*—ate [polite past form of 食べる (to eat)]

酒 *sake*—alcohol; alcoholic beverage; *sake*

を *o*—(indicates the direct object of action)

飲みません *nomimasen*—don't drink [polite negative for of 飲む (to drink)]

よんでみよう！LET'S READ!

Learn through reading for (very) beginners of Japanese

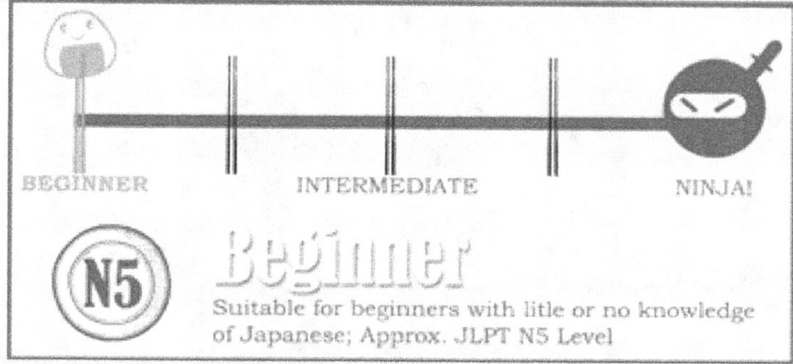

Have you only recently learned hiragana but need practice? Or perhaps, your hiragana is no problem, but you want to build your reading comprehension?

This segment is here to the rescue!

Read real Japanese—beginner level but not boring Japanese! Enjoy reading flash fiction, super short essays, and funny stories of common mistakes made by foreigners in Japan.

Best of all, the only requirement is that you can read hiragana. Vocabulary and grammar will be defined and explained.

The format is a little different from our other more advanced readers. The idea is for the reader to read the entire story three times. Each page will have a sentence or two in hiragana (with spaces between words for you to see "words" instead of syllables) at the top and that same content in full Japanese (with furigana) at the bottom. The middle will have the glossary and grammatical explanations. Lastly, the story will be presented in Japanese without furigana. See if you can read it after going through the explanations.

If you have just learned hiragana, you may want to listen to the sound file while reading the hiragana section to practice correct pronunciation. If you have studied Japanese a bit longer, you may want to start with the bottom version and take note of the glossary for understanding.

Makoto+ members can access this in a more interactive format. To learn more:

http://MakotoPlus.com

And now…

Let's learn about…

JAPANESE STREET FOOD

PART 1: "TAKOYAKI"

Normal Speed

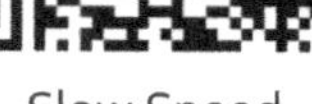

Slow Speed

Normal Speed

Slow Speed

The top and bottom Japanese texts are identical in meaning. The top version is only in hiragana and includes spaces between words. The bottom version has no spaces and uses kanji with furigana. Unless you are just practicing hiragana recognition, try to work through both versions. Scan the QR codes for the sound files.

日本のストリートフード　その１

「たこ焼き」

JAPANESE STREET FOOD, PART 1

"TAKOYAKI"

にほん　の　すとりーと　ふーど　は　たくさん　あります。その
だいひょう　と　いえば、たこやき。

GLOSSARY AND NOTES

日本のストリートフード *nihon no sutori-to fu-do*—street food in Japan; street food of Japan; Japanese street food [日本 (Japan) + の (of; in; 's; modifier) + ストリートフード (street food)]

その1 *sono ichi*—Part 1

は *wa*—(indicates the sentence topic)

たくさんあります *takusan arimasu*—there are many; have many; have a lot [たくさん (many; a lot; much; plenty; lots; a large number) + あります (have; ます/polite form of ある (to have; to be; to exist))]

その代表と言えば *sono daihyou to ieba*—one of the best examples; speaking of a representative example (of Japanese street food) [その (the; that) + 代表 (representative example; representation; model) + と言えば (speaking of; when you talk of; how to form: Noun + と言えば)]

たこ焼き *takoyaki*—takoyaki; octopus dumplings [たこ (octopus) + 焼き (frying or stir-frying; heating)]

日本のストリートフードはたくさんあります。その代表と言えば、たこ焼き。

たこやき は、ひとくち さいず の まるい ぼーる がた の た
べもの。なか に は たこ の ぶつぎり が はいっています。お
さら に ろっこ から じゅっこ くらい はいっています。

GLOSSARY AND NOTES

たこ焼きは *takoyaki wa—takoyaki*; octopus dumplings [たこ (octopus) + 焼き (frying or stir-frying; heating) + は (indicates the sentence topic)]

一口サイズの丸いボール型の食べ物 *hitokuchi saizu no marui bo-ru gata no tabemono*—a bite-sized, round, ball-shaped food [一口 (mouthful; a bite; one bite; 一 (one) + 口 (mouth)) + サイズ (size) + の (of; modifier) + 丸い (round; circular; spherical) + ボール (ball) + 型 (form; shape; mold) + の (of; modifier) + 食べ物 (food)]

中には *naka ni wa*—in the; inside [中 (inside; interior) + に (in; expresses the location of existence) + は (adds emphasis)]

たこのぶつ切りが入っています *tako no butsugiri ga haitte imasu*—is filled with chunk of octopus [たこ (octopus) + の (of; modifier) + ぶつ切り (chunk; lump; cutting into chunks; thick slice) + が (identifies what performs the action; emphasizes the preceding word) + 入っています (ています-form of 入る (to contain; to get in) which is used to describe the actual condition or appearance of the subject; how to form: Verb て-form + います)]

お皿に *osara ni*—in the plate [お皿 (plate; dish; お is an honorific/polite/humble prefix) + に (in; expresses the location of existence)]

6個から10個くらい *rokko kara jukko kurai*—about 6 to 10 pieces [6個 (6 pieces; 個 is counter for articles) + から (from) + 10個 (10 pieces) + くらい (approximately; about; around; or so)]

入っています *haitteimasu*—is contained; contain [ています-form of 入る (to contain; to have) which is used to describe the actual condition or appearance of the subject]

たこ焼きは、一口サイズの丸いボール型の食べ物。中にはたこのぶ
つ切りが入っています。お皿に6個から10個くらい入っています。

あまめ　の　しょうゆ　べーす　の　そーす　と　まよねーず、かつお
ぶし、あお　のり　など　を　かけて　たべます。おみせ　に　よっ
て、あじ　が　ちがいます。これ　も　おもしろい　です。

GLOSSARY AND NOTES

甘めの醤油ベースのソース *amame no shouyu be-su no so-su*—sweetish soy sauce-based sauce [甘め (sweetish; somewhat sweet) + の (modifier) + 醤油 (soy sauce) + ベース (base; basic ingredient; basis) + の (of; modifier) + ソース (sauce)]

と *to*—and

マヨネーズ *mayone-zu*—mayonnaise

かつおぶし *katsuobushi*—bonito flakes; small pieces of sliced dried bonito; *katsuobushi*

青のりなど *ao nori nado*—green laver, etc. [青のり (green laver; green dried seaweed; *nori*) + など (etc.; and so forth; and the like; and others)]

を *o*—(indicates the direct object of action)

かけて食べます *kakete tabemasu*—is eaten after brushing (with sauce); top (with sauce) and eat [かけて (て-form of かける (to put on top of; to spread) which is used to connect to the next verb) + 食べます (eat; ます/polite form of 食べる (to eat))]

お店によって *omise ni yotte*—(differ) from one restaurant to another; (differ) depending on the store [お店 (restaurant; store; shop) + によって (depending on; something is different depending on the preceding noun; how to form: Noun + によって)]

味が違います *aji ga chigaimasu*—the taste differs [味 (taste; flavor) + が (identifies what performs the action) + 違います (ます/polite form of 違う (to differ (from); to vary))]

これも *kore mo*—this also; this is also [これ (this; this one) + も (also; too; as well)]

面白い *omoshiroi*—interesting; fascinating; enthralling

です *desu*—be; is

甘めの醤油ベースのソースとマヨネーズ、かつおぶし、青のりなどを
かけて食べます。お店によって、味が違います。これも面白いです。

たこ　が　にがてな　ひと　は、「たこぬき」で　ちゅうもん　でき
ます。たこやき　は　おおさか　から　はじまりました　が、いま
は　にほん　ぜんこく、どこ　でも　たべられます。

GLOSSARY AND NOTES

たこが苦手な人は *tako ga nigatena hito wa*—people who don't like octopus [たこ　(octopus) + が (emphasizes the preceding word) + 苦手な (not one's favorite; not like) + 人 (person; people) + は (indicates the sentence topic)]

「たこ抜き」「*takonuki*」—"*takonuki* (without octopus)" [「」 (quotation marks; " ") + たこ (*tako*; octopus) + 抜き (omitting; skipping; leaving out; without; with no...)]

「たこ抜き」で注文できます「*takonuki*」 *de chuumon dekimasu*—can order (it) with "*takonuki*" [「たこ抜き」 ("*takonuki* (without octopus)") + で (with; by; indicates means of action) + 注文 (order (for an item)) + できます (can do; to be able to do; ます/polite form of できる (potential form of する (to do)))]

大阪から *oosaka kara*—from Osaka [大阪 (Osaka (city; prefecture of Japan)) + から (from)]

始まりました *hajimarimashita*—started [polite past form of 始まる (to start; to begin)]

が *ga*—but; however

今は *ima wa*—now [今 (now; the present time) + は (adds emphasis)]

日本全国 *nihon zenkoku*—all over Japan; throughout Japan [日本 (Japan) + 全 (all; whole; entire) + 国 (country; state)]

どこでも *doko demo*—anywhere; anyplace; everywhere

食べられます *taberaremasu*—can eat; can have [polite potential positive form of 食べる (to eat; to have)]

たこが苦手な人は、「たこ抜き」で注文できます。たこ焼きは大阪から始まりましたが、今は日本全国、どこでも食べられます。

日本のストリートフード　その１
「たこ焼き」
JAPANESE STREET FOOD, PART 1
"TAKOYAKI"

Now, let's read the story once more in natural Japanese.
Lastly, check the English translation to make sure you understand.

　日本のストリートフードはたくさんあります。その代表と言えば、たこ焼き。たこ焼きは、一口サイズの丸いボール型の食べ物。中にはたこのぶつ切りが入っています。お皿に6個から10個くらい入っています。甘めの醤油ベースのソースとマヨネーズ、かつおぶし、青のりなどをかけて食べます。お店によって、味が違います。これも面白いです。たこが苦手な人は、「たこ抜き」で注文できます。たこ焼きは大阪から始まりましたが、今は日本全国、どこでも食べられます。

ENGLISH: (try to save this for last)

There are many types of street food in Japan. One of the best examples is *takoyaki* (octopus dumplings). *Takoyaki* is a bite-sized, round, ball-shaped food. It is filled with chunks of octopus. There are about 6 to 10 pieces per plate. They are eaten after brushing them with a sweetish soy sauce-based sauce and mayonnaise, and sprinkling with bonito flakes, green laver (green dried seaweed), etc. The taste differs from one restaurant to another. This is also interesting. People who don't like octopus, can order it with "*takonuki* (without octopus)". *Takoyaki* started from Osaka, but now you can have it anywhere throughout Japan.

KEY VOCABULARY	

日本のストリートフード *nihon no sutori-to fu-do*—street food in Japan; Japanese street food	マヨネーズ *mayone-zu*—mayonnaise
たこ焼き *takoyaki—takoyaki*; octopus dumplings	たこ抜き *takonuki— takonuki* (without octopus)
甘めの醤油ベースのソース *amame no shouyu be-su no so-su*—sweetish soy sauce-based sauce	大阪から *oosaka*—Osaka
かつおぶし *katsuobushi*—bonito fish flakes	日本全国 *nihon zenkoku*—throughout Japan; all over Japan [日本 (Japan) + 全 (all; whole; entire) + 国 (country; state)]

JAPANESE READER

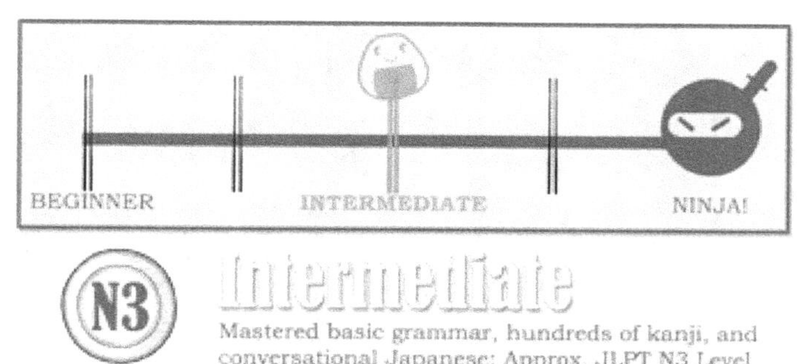

N3 **Intermediate**
Mastered basic grammar, hundreds of kanji, and
conversational Japanese; Approx. JLPT N3 Level

きっちょむさんと餅屋の主人

Kicchomu and the Owner of the Rice Cake Shop

Story Read Normal

Story Read Slow Speed

Work through the story, sentence-by-sentence, referring to the vocabulary and grammar explanations below as needed.

むかしむかし、きっちょむさんという面白い人がいました。ある日、きっちょむさんは、たきぎを売ろうと思って馬の背中にたきぎを積んで、村にでかけました。

餅屋の主人 owner of the rice cake shop [餅屋 (rice cake shop (store)) + の (of; modifier) + 主人 (owner; master; host)]

むかしむかし long ago; once upon a time

きっちょむさんという named Kicchomu [きっちょむさん (Kicchomu; さん is an honorific suffix which means Mr., Mrs., or Miss that can be used with both first and last names and both genders) + という (named; is used to define, describe, and generally just talk about the thing itself)]

面白い人 interesting man [面白い (interesting; fascinating; enthralling) + 人 (man; person; people)]

(が)いました there was/were [polite past form of (が)いる (there is/are; to be (living things)); how to form: Noun + (が)いました]

ある日 one day; (on) a certain day [ある (a certain; some) + 日 (day)]

きっちょむさんは Kicchomu [きっちょむさん (Kicchomu) + は (indicates the sentence topic)]

たきぎを売ろうと思って hoping to sell the firewood; thinking to sell the firewood [たきぎ (piece(s) of firewood (especially chopped or split from logs); firewood) + を (indicates the direct object of action) + 売ろう (plain volitional form of 売る (to sell); volitional form of a verb is used when the speaker initiates an act) + と思って (て-form of と思う (to think...; I think...; you think...; is used to describe your own thoughts or someone else's thoughts) which is used to connect to the next phrase)]

馬の背中に on the horse's back [馬 (horse) + の (of; 's; modifier) + 背中 (back (of body)) + に (on; expresses the location of existence)]

たきぎを積んで load the firewood [たきぎ (firewood) + を (indicates たきぎ as the direct object of action) + 積んで (て-form of 積む (to load; to stack; to pile up) which is used to connect to the next phrase)]

村にでかけました went out to the village [村 (village) + に (to; expresses the direction and destination) + でかけました (went out; polite past form of でかける (to go out; to leave; to depart; to set out))]

「たきぎはいらんかね〜？たきぎはいらんかね〜？」と、村の

中を歩いていきました。すると、餅屋の主人がきっちょむさん

に聞きました。「きっちょむさん、それは全部でいくらか

ね？」

「」(quotation marks; " ")

たきぎはいらんかね〜？ Do (you) need firewood? [た
きぎ (firewood) + は (as for the (firewood); contrast
marker) + いらん (is a colloquial form of いらない
(plain negative form of いる (to need; to want))) + か
ね (interrogative sentence-ending particle expressing
doubt)]

と (quotation marker)

村の中を歩いていきました walked through the village [
村 (village) + の (modifier; is used to tell the location) + 中 (in; inside; through) + を (indicates the
direct object of action) + 歩いていきました (walked
and went (somewhere); ～ていきました is the polite
past form of ～ていく (describes a motion going away
from the place where the speaker is); how to form:
Verb て-form + いきました)]

すると and; then [can be used to begin a sentence or
clause]

餅屋の主人が the owner of the rice cake shop [餅屋
(rice cake shop) + の (of; 's; modifier) + 主人 (owner)
+ が (identifies who performs the action)]

きっちょむさんに聞きました asked Kicchomu [きっ
ちょむさん (Kicchomu) + に (expresses the object of
the verb) + 聞きました (asked; polite past form of 聞
く (to ask; to enquire))]

それは that [それ (that; it) + は (adds emphasis)]

全部で altogether; all in all; in total; overall [全部 (all;
altogether; entire) + で (in; indicates a total amount
of something)]

いくらかね？ How much? [いくら (how much) + かね
(interrogative sentence-ending particle expressing
doubt)]

きっちょむさんは、馬の背中に積んだたきぎのことだと思い、

こう言いました。「全部ですか？全部なら100文です。」

「１００文か。それなら買おう。ここに100文あるぞ。」

馬の背中に積んだ loaded on the horse's back [馬 (horse) + の ('s; of; modifier) + 背中 (back (of body)) + に (on; expresses the location of existence) + 積んだ (loaded; plain past form of 積む (to load; to pile up; to stack))]

たきぎのこと all the things about the firewood [たきぎ (firewood) + のこと (all the things about; it has a "focusing" feature and lets you know that the subject has a certain quality; how to form: Noun + のこと)]

だと思い thinking; think and [ます-stem form of だと思う (to think...; I think...; you think...; how to form: Noun + だ + と思う); which is used to connect to the next phrase; connecting verbs with ます-stem is more formal]

こう言いました said; said so [polite past form of こう言う (say so); こう (refers to what the speaker has said) + 言いました (polite past form of 言う (to say; to utter))]

全部ですか？ All? [全部 (all; entire; whole; altogether) + です (be; is) + か (indicates a question)]

全部なら if all (of it) [全部 (all) + なら (if; in case; if it is the case that)]

100文です it's one hundred *mon* [100文 (one hundred *mon*; 文 (one-thousandth of a *kan* (Japan's unit of currency 1336-1870))) + です (be; is)]

100文か hmm, one hundred *mon* [100文 (one hundred *mon*) + か (hmm; expresses the speaker's uncertainty about something)]

それなら then; if that's the case ...; if so ... [それ (that; it) + なら (if; in case; if it is the case that)]

買おう I'll buy [plain volitional form of 買う (to buy; to purchase) which is used when the speaker initiates an act]

ここに here [ここ (here; now) + に (expresses the location of existence)]

ここに100文あるぞ here's a hundred *mon* [ここに (here) + 100文 (hundred *mon*) + ある (to be; to have) + ぞ (sentence ender that adds force spoken by males)]

きっちょむさんは、喜んで代金を受け取りました。餅屋の主人
は、「代金は払ったからもらっていくぞ。」と言って、たきぎを
積んだ馬を連れて行こうとしました。

喜んで gladly; with pleasure … [て-form (adverbial form) of 喜ぶ (to be glad; to be delighted) which is used to modify the verb 受け取りました (accepted)]

代金を受け取りました accepted the payment [代金 (payment; fee; cost; price; charge) + を (indicates the direct object of action) + 受け取りました (accepted; polite past form of 受け取る (to accept; to receive; to get))]

餅屋の主人は the owner of the rice cake shop [餅屋 (rice cake shop) + の (of; 's; modifier) + 主人 (owner) + は (indicates the sentence topic)]

代金は払ったから paid the price, so [代金 (payment; fee; cost; price; charge) + は (as for the (price); contrast marker) + 払った (paid; plain past form of 払う (to pay)) + から (so; because; since)]

もらっていく to take (it) and go (somewhere) [もらって (て-form of もらう (to take; to receive) which is used to connect to the next verb いく) + いく (to move (in a direction or towards a specific location); to go); ~ていく is used to describe a motion going away from the place where the speaker is]

ぞ (sentence ender that adds force spoken by males)

と言って said and [と (quotation marker) + 言って (て-form of 言う (to say; to utter; to declare) which is used to connect to the next phrase, creating the meaning of "and")]

たきぎを積んだ馬 the horse that was loaded with firewood [たきぎ (firewood) + を (indicates the direct object of action) + 積んだ (loaded; plain past form of 積む (to load; to pile up; to stack)) + 馬 (horse)]

たきぎを積んだ馬を連れて行こうとしました was about to take the horse that was loaded with firewood [たきぎを積んだ馬 (the horse that was loaded with firewood) + を (indicates the direct object of action) + 連れて行こうとしました (was about to take; 連れて行こう (plain volitional form of 連れて行く (to take (someone to a place); to take along)); 「Verb (volitional form) + としました」 means "was about to do ~; tried to do ~")]

きっちょむさんは慌てて餅屋の主人を止めました。「たきぎは全部売りましたが、馬は売っていません。連れて行かないでください。」「何？ 私は馬も入れて「全部でいくらだ？」と聞いたんだ。

慌てて hurriedly; hastily; in a hurry; in a mad rush; in haste; hurry and [て-form (adverbial form) of 慌てる (to hurry; to rush; to hasten) which is used to express how the action 止めました (stopped) takes place]

餅屋の主人を止めました stopped the owner of the rice cake shop [餅屋の主人 (owner of the rice cake shop) + を (indicates the direct object of action) + 止めました (stopped; polite past form of 止める (to stop))]

たきぎは全部売りました sold all the firewood [たきぎ (firewood) + は (as for the (firewood); contrast marker) + 全部 (all; entire; altogether) + 売りました (sold; polite past form of 売る (to sell))]

が but; however

馬は売っていません not selling the horse [馬 (horse) + は (as for the (horse); contrast marker) + 売っていません (not selling; from 売る (to sell); ~ていません is the polite negative form of ~ている (describes an ongoing action); how to form: Verb て-form + いません)]

連れて行かないでください please don't take (the horse) [from 連れて行く (to take along); ~ないでください means "please don't do" which is used after a verb to request to the listener to not do something; how to form: Verb (ない form) + で + ください]

何？ What?

私は I [私 (I; me) + は (indicates the sentence topic)]

馬も入れて including the horse also [馬 (horse) + も (also) + 入れて (including; て-form of 入れる (to include; to put in) which is used to connect to the next phrase)]

「全部でいくらだ？」 "How much for everything?" [「」 (quotation marks; " ") + 全部 (all; every bit; everything; the entirety) + で (indicates a total amount of something) + いくら (how much) + だ (assertive; used to emphasize your sentence)]

「全部でいくらだ？」と聞いたんだ (I) asked, "How much for everything?" [「全部でいくらだ？」 ("How much for everything?") + と (quotation marker) + 聞いた (asked; plain past form of 聞く (to ask; to enquire)) + んだ (is used to show emphasis; is very casual and often used in conversation with close friends and family members)]

もう代金は払ったんだから、馬ももらうぞ。」と言って、馬を
連れて行ってしまいました。 きっちょむさんは、とても悔しく
思って、仕返ししてやろうと考えました。

もう already

代金は払ったん paid for the price [代金 (price; payment; charge) + は (as for the (price); contrast marker) + 払った (paid; plain past form of 払う (to pay)) + ん (casual form of の (explanatory particle))]

だから so; therefore; for that reason

馬ももらうぞ (I) take the horse too [馬 (horse) + も (too; also) + もらう (to take; to receive) + ぞ (sentence ender that adds force spoken by males)]

と言って said and [と (quotation marker) + 言って (て-form of 言う (to say; to utter) which is used to connect to the next phrase, creating the meaning of "and")]

馬を連れて行ってしまいました took the horse away [馬 (horse) + を (indicates 馬 as the direct object of action) + 連れて行ってしまいました (took away; from 連れて行く (take away; lead off; bring along); ~てしまいました is the polite past form of ~てしまう (refers to a regrettable event or negative meaning); how to form: Verb て-form + しまいました)]

とても悔しく思って (Kicchomu) felt so frustrated [とても (so; very; so much) + 悔しく (continuative/adverbial form of 悔しい (deeply regret; frustrating; bitter) which is used to describe how he felt; 思って describes what you feel or think of the object of the verb) + 思って (て-form of 思う (to feel; to think) which is used to connect to the next phrase)]

仕返ししてやろうと考えました decided to get even [仕返ししてやろう (from 仕返しする (have one's revenge; get even; retaliate); ~てやろう is the plain volitional form of ~てやる (is used to express very harsh actions); volitional form of a verb is used when the speaker initiates an act) + と (is used for quoting thoughts) + 考えました (polite past form of 考える (to intend (to do); to think))]

その日の夕方、餅屋の主人がお店で働いていると、きっちょむ

さんがやってきました。「お〜、忙しそうだね。なかなかいい

店だ。いくらだ？」きっちょむさんは、忙しそうに働いてい

る主人に後ろから聞きました。

その日の夕方 that evening; the same evening [その (that; the) + 日 (day) + の (of; modifier) + 夕方 (evening; dusk)]

お店で働いていると when the (the owner of the rice cake shop) is working at (his) store [お店 (store; shop) + で (at; indicates the location of action) + 働いている (is working; ている-form of 働く (to work; to labor) which is used to describe an ongoing action; how to form: Verb て-form + いる) + と (when)]

きっちょむさんがやってきました Kicchomu came by [きっちょむさん (Kicchomu) + が (identifies who performs the action) + やってきました (came by; polite past form of やってくる (to come along; to come around; to come by))]

お〜 oh; ooh

忙しそうだね (you) seem to be busy [忙しそう (from 忙しい (busy; occupied; hectic); 〜そう means "seems like 〜; looks like 〜"; how to form: い-adjective + ⇥ + そう) + だ (casual form of the polite copula です (be; is)) + ね (sentence ender which is used on the assumption that the speaker and the listener have the same feelings and information in common)]

なかなかいい店だ it's quite a nice store [なかなか (quite; considerably; fairly) + いい (nice; good; fine) + 店 (store; shop) + だ (casual form of the polite copula です (be; is))]

いくらだ how much is (it)? [いくら (how much) + だ (be; is)]

忙しそうに働いている主人に (asked) the owner who is busily working [忙しそうに (busily; に is added after 忙しそう to turn it into an adverbial form) + 働いている (is working; ている-form of 働く (to work; to labor) which is used to describe an ongoing action) + 主人 (owner) + に (expresses the object of the verb)]

後ろから from behind [後ろ (behind; back; rear) + から (from)]

聞きました asked [polite past form of 聞く (to ask; to enquire; to query)]

餅屋の主人は、ほかのお客さんに餅を渡しながら、後ろ向きのまま、返事をしました。「ああ、２０文です。」 「安いな。買ったぞ。」 「はい、ありがとうございます。」

ほかのお客さんに to other customers [ほかの (other; another) + お客さん (customer; client; shopper) + に (to; expresses the direction)]

餅を渡しながら while handing out rice cakes [餅 ((sticky) rice cake; *mochi*) + を (indicates the direct object of action) + 渡しながら (from 渡す (to hand over; to hand in); ~ながら means "while; during; as; simultaneously"; how to form: Verb ます (stem form) + ながら)]

後ろ向きのまま remained facing backward [後ろ (back; behind; rear) + 向き (direction) + のまま (as it is; without changing ~; current state; how to form: Noun + の + まま)]

返事をしました replied [polite past form of 返事をする (reply; give an answer; respond)]

ああ ah; yup

20文です is twenty *mon* [20文 (twenty *mon*) + です (be; is)]

安い cheap; inexpensive

な (casual suffix) [is used when you express your opinion or feeling; is generally considered to be "male speech"]

買ったぞ (I) bought (it) [買った (plain past form of 買う (to buy; to purchase)) + ぞ (sentence ender that adds force spoken by males)]

はい yes

ありがとうございます thank you

餅屋の主人が代金を受け取って振り返ると、そこにはきっちょ
むさんが立っていました。「馬は返さないぞ。」「馬はいらな
い。この店を買ったんだ。早く出て行けよ。」

代金を受け取って振り返ると when the (owner of the rice cake shop) takes the payment and turns around [代金 (payment; cost; fee) + を (indicates the direct object of action) + 受け取って (take and; て-form of 受け取る (to take; to receive; to accept) which is used to connect to the next phrase, creating the meaning of "and") + 振り返る (to turn around) + と (when)]

そこにはきっちょむさんが立っていました Kicchomu was standing there [そこ (there) + には (puts more emphasis and restriction on the preceding word; に (expresses the location of existence) + は (adds emphasis)) + きっちょむさん (Kicchomu) + が (identifies who performs the action) + 立っていました (was standing; ていました-form of 立つ (to stand) which is used to describe a continuous action happening in the past)]

馬は返さないぞ (I) won't give (you) back the horse; (I) will not return the horse [馬 (horse) + は (as for the (horse); contrast marker) + 返さない (do not return; plain negative form of 返す (to return (something); to put back; to restore)) + ぞ (sentence ender that adds force spoken by males)]

馬はいらない (I) don't need the horse [馬 (horse) + は (as for the (horse); contrast marker) + いらない (plain negative form of いる (to need; to want))]

この店を買ったんだ (I) bought this store [この (this) + 店 (store; shop) + を (indicates the direct object of action) + 買った (bought; plain past form of 買う (to buy; to purchase)) + ん (casual form of の (explanatory particle)) + だ (casual form of the polite copula です (be; is))]

早く quickly; swiftly [adverbial form of 早い (quick; fast; swift)]

出て行け get out [plain imperative form of 出て行く (to go out and away; to leave)]

よ (sentence ender showing emphasis and certainty)

「なに？店など売ってないぞ。」「いや、さっき、いくらだ？

と聞いたら、お前は２０文と言ったじゃないか。俺は店の値段

を聞いたんだ。２０文払ったんだ。

なに？ What?

店など store, etc. [店 (store; shop; restaurant) + など (et cetera; etc.; and so forth; and the like)]

売ってないぞ is not sold; is not selling; don't sell [売ってない (from 売る (to sell); 〜てない is the casual form of 〜ていない (plain negative form of 〜ている (describes an ongoing action)) which is used in conversation) + ぞ (sentence ender that adds force spoken by males)]

いや no; nay

さっき a short while ago; a moment ago; just now

いくらだ？ How much? [いくら (how much) + だ (casual form of the polite copula です (be; is))]

いくらだ？と聞いたら when (I) asked, "How much?" [いくらだ？ (how much?) + と (used for quoting speech) + 聞いたら (when (I) asked; from 聞く (to ask; to enquire); 〜たら means "if; when 〜; after"; how to form: Verb (た form) + ら)]

お前 you [male term or language; formerly honorific, now an often derogatory term referring to an equal or inferior]

20文と言った you said, "Twenty *mon*." [20文 (twenty *mon*) + と (used for quoting speech) + 言った (said; plain past form of 言う (to say; to utter; to declare))]

じゃないか right?; isn't it? [questioning (something)]

俺 I; me [male term or language, rough or arrogant]

店の値段を聞いたんだ asked the shop's price [店 (shop; store) + の ('s; of; modifier) + 値段 (price; cost) + を (indicates the direct object of action) + 聞いた (asked; plain past form of 聞く (to ask; to enquire)) + んだ (casual form of のです (explanatory ender) which is used to indicate that the statement being made is based on background information or knowledge shared by the speaker and the listener)]

20文払ったんだ paid twenty *mon* [20文 (twenty *mon*) + 払った (paid; plain past form of 払う (to pay)) + んだ (casual explanatory ender)]

お前は、代金をうけとっただろう？さ、出ていけ。」餅屋の

主人は、きっちょむさんに一生懸命に謝って、馬を返してあ

げました。そして、山盛りの餅もあげたそうです。おしまい。

代金をうけとった (you) got the payment [代金 (price; payment; cost) + を (indicates the direct object of action) + うけとった (got; plain past form of うけとる (to get; to receive; to accept))]

だろう right?; don't you agree?

さ well; now

出ていけ get out; leave [plain imperative form of 出ていく (to go out and away; to leave)]

きっちょむさんに to Kicchomu [きっちょむさん (Kicchomu) + に (to; expresses the object of the verb)]

一生懸命に謝って heartily apologize and [一生懸命に (heartily; with all of one's strength; with heart and soul; に is added to turn 一生懸命 (with utmost effort; eagerly; very hard) into its adverbial form) + 謝って (apologize and; て-form of 謝る (to apologize) which is used to connect to the next phrase, creating the meaning of "and")]

馬を返してあげました gave back the horse [馬 (horse) + を (indicates the direct object of action) + 返してあげました (from 返す (to return (something); to restore); ～てあげました is the polite past form of ～てあげる (to do for; to do a favor); how to form: Verb て-form + あげました)]

そして and

山盛りの餅もあげた (he) also gave (him) a heap of rice cakes [山盛り (heap; pile; stack) + の (of; modifier) + 餅 (mochi; (sticky) rice cake) + も (also; too) + あげた (gave; plain past form of あげる (to give))]

そうです it is said that ~; (I) heard that ~ [how to form: Verb (casual form) + そうです]

おしまい the end

Kicchomu and the Owner of the Rice Cake Shop

Please try to tackle the Japanese first and use this only as needed.

Once upon a time, there was an interesting man named Kicchomu.

One day, Kicchomu went out to the village with a load of firewood on his horse's back, hoping to sell it. Kicchomu shouted out, "Do you need firewood? Do you need firewood?" as he walked through the village.

Then, the owner of the rice cake shop asked Kicchomu, "How much for everything, Kicchomu?"

Thinking he was talking about the pile of firewood on the horse's back, Kicchomu said, "All? If all of it, it's one hundred *mon*."

"Hmm, one hundred *mon*. I'll buy it then. Here's a hundred *mon*."

Kicchomu gladly accepted the payment.

The owner of the rice cake shop said, "I've paid you, so I'll take it.", and was about to take the horse that was loaded with firewood. Kicchomu hurriedly stopped the owner of the rice cake shop.

"I've sold all the firewood, but not the horse. Please don't take him."

"What? I asked, 'How much for everything?' including the horse also. I've already paid for the price, so I'll take the horse too," said the owner of the rice cake shop, and he took the horse away.

Kicchomu felt so frustrated that he decided to get even. That evening, when the owner of the rice cake shop was working at his store, Kicchomu came by.

Kicchomu asked the owner, who was busily working, from behind, "Oh, you seem to be busy. It's quite a nice store. How much is it?"

The owner of the rice cake shop, while handing out rice cakes to other customers, who remained facing backward, replied, "Ah, it's twenty mon."

"That's cheap. I'll take it."

"Yes, thank you."

When the owner of the rice cake shop took the payment and turned around, he saw Kicchomu standing there.

"I won't give you back the horse."

Continued

"I don't need the horse. I bought this store. Get out of here quickly."

"What? I didn't sell the store, etc."

"No, just now, when I asked, 'How much is it?' you said, 'Twenty *mon*,' right? I asked you the shop's price. I paid twenty *mon*. You got the payment, right? Now, get out of here."

The owner of the rice cake shop heartily apologized to Kicchomu and gave him back his horse. And it was said that he also gave him a heap of rice cakes.

The End.

きっちょむさんと餅屋の主人

むかしむかし、きっちょむさんという面白い人がいました。

ある日、きっちょむさんは、たきぎを売ろうと思って馬の背中にたきぎを積んで、村にでかけました。

「たきぎはいらんかね〜？たきぎはいらんかね〜？」と、村の中を歩いていきました。

すると、餅屋の主人がきっちょむさんに聞きました。

「きっちょむさん、それは全部でいくらかね？」

きっちょむさんは、馬の背中に積んだたきぎのことだと思い、こう言いました。

「全部ですか？全部なら100文です。」

「１００文か。それなら買おう。ここに100文あるぞ。」

きっちょむさんは、喜んで代金を受け取りました。

餅屋の主人は、「代金は払ったからもらっていくぞ。」と言って、たきぎを積んだ馬を連れて行こうとしました。きっちょむさんは慌てて餅屋の主人を止めました。

「たきぎは全部売りましたが、馬は売っていません。連れて行かないでください。」

「何？私は馬も入れて「全部でいくらだ？」と聞いたんだ。もう代金は払ったんだから、馬ももらうぞ。」と言って、馬を連れて行ってしまいました。

きっちょむさんは、とても悔しく思って、仕返ししてやろうと考えました。その日の夕方、餅屋の主人がお店で働いていると、きっちょむさんがやってきました。

Continued

「お〜、忙しそうだね。なかなかいい店だ。いくらだ？」きっちょむさんは、忙しそうに働いている主人に後ろから聞きました。

餅屋の主人は、ほかのお客さんに餅を渡しながら、後ろ向きのまま、返事をしました。

「ああ、20文です。」

「安いな。買ったぞ。」

「はい、ありがとうございます。」

餅屋の主人が代金を受け取って振り返ると、そこにはきっちょむさんが立っていました。

「馬は返さないぞ。」

「馬はいらない。この店を買ったんだ。早く出て行けよ。」

「なに？店など売ってないぞ。」

「いや、さっき、いくらだ？と聞いたら、お前は20文と言ったじゃないか。俺は店の値段を聞いたんだ。20文払ったんだ。お前は、代金をうけとっただろう？さ、出ていけ。」

餅屋の主人は、きっちょむさんに一生懸命に謝って、馬を返してあげました。そして、山盛りの餅もあげたそうです。

おしまい。

Kanji in Focus

It is usually helpful to create a story based on the meanings of the kanji parts. Often, different kanji learning systems will use different "meanings" for the parts. We try to give the most common ones, but consistency is best. Choose one meaning per kanji part and stick with it. The following are a selection of the kanji found in this story. The <u>underlined</u> reading is probably the most used.

背	**READINGS**	<u>ハイ</u>・<u>せ</u>・せい・そむく・そむける	北 north
	MEANING	stature; height; back	月 moon; month
	EXAMPLE	背中 back (of body)	She'll travel *back* to the **north** 北 part of the world next **month** 月.

積	**READINGS**	<u>セキ</u>・<u>つむ</u>・~づみ・つもる・つもり	禾 grain
			十 ten; 10
	MEANING	pile up; stack; load	二 two; 2
			貝 shellfish; seashell; shell
	EXAMPLE	積む to pile up; to stack	*Load* the sacks of **grain** 禾 to **ten** 十 huge containers including these **2** 二 bags of **shellfish** 貝.

餅	**READINGS**	ヘイ・ヒョウ・<u>もち</u>・もちい	食 eat; food
			ヽ sparks
	MEANING	*mochi*; (sticky) rice cake	开 in Chinese, this is a simplified version of 開 (to open)
	EXAMPLE	餅屋 rice cake shop keeper; rice cake store (shop)	When he **eats** 食 *mochi*, his eyes **spark** ヽ and **open** 开 so wide.

馬	**READINGS**	バ・<u>うま</u>・うま~・ま	｜ line; vertical stroke; rod
			三 three; 3
	MEANING	horse	㇆ backward tip of a hook
			灬 fire
	EXAMPLE	馬 horse; horse racing	The *horse* leads him to a place where a **rod** ｜ and **three** 三 types of **backward tip of a hook** ㇆ are on **fire** 灬.

慌	**READINGS**	<u>コウ</u>・<u>あわてる</u>・あわ ただしい	忄 heart
			艹 grass; herb; plant
	MEANING	disconcerted; be confused; lose one's head	亡 death
			川 river; stream
	EXAMPLE	慌てる to panic; to hurry	Don't *be confused* when the **heart** 忄 of a **plant** 艹 is facing **death** 亡 while it floats on the **river** 川.

後	**READINGS** **MEANING** **EXAMPLE**	ゴ・コウ・のち・うし ろ・あと・おくれる behind; back; later うし 後ろ behind; rear; back	彳 step 幺 short; tiny 夂 go They **step** 彳 forward to pick up the **tiny** 幺 stone ring before they **go** 夂 *back* home.
返	**READINGS** **MEANING** **EXAMPLE**	ヘン・かえす・~かえ す・かえる・~かえる return; answer; fade; repay かえ 返す to return (something); to restore	辶 walk; road; advance 厂 cliff 又 again; once more; once again I want to *return* to that **road** 辶 heading towards a **cliff** 厂, **once again** 又.
買	**READINGS** **MEANING** **EXAMPLE**	バイ・かう buy か　もの 買い物 shopping; pur- chased goods	罒 net 貝 shellfish; seashell; shell You need to *buy* a **net** 罒 bag for your **seashell** 貝 collection.
懸	**READINGS** **MEANING** **EXAMPLE**	ケン・ケ・かける・か かる state of suspension; hang; depend; consult; distant; far apart いっしょうけんめい 一生懸命 very hard; with utmost effort	目 eye; eyeball 乚 an L 小 small 丿 a stroke curved to the left 糸 thread; yarn; string 心 heart; mind; spirit You should have an **eye** 目 on that **L** 乚 shaped, **small** 小 objects with **a stroke curved to the left** 丿, that *hang* on the wall by a **thread** 糸, and keep them in your **mind** 心.
盛	**READINGS** **MEANING** **EXAMPLE**	セイ・ジョウ・もる・ さかる・さかん boom; prosper やまも 山盛り heap; pile; stack;	成 become; reach; turn 皿 plate; dish; platter When you *prosper* and **become** 成 rich, you can afford to buy this **plate** 皿 made of gold.

Do you have any questions? Anything confusing? Feel free to email me (Clay) at clay@thejapanshop.com with any questions, comments, or suggestions.

Do you have ideas to make *Makoto* better? We'd love to hear from you. Did something particularly help you? Love to hear that as well.

What to experience even more Makoto? Learn about our new Makoto+ membership. Download the latest issue or access web-based back issues. All this and more starting at only $3. Go to: **www.MakotoPlus.com** now!

Clay & Yumi